IMAGES
of America

VALLEY FORGE

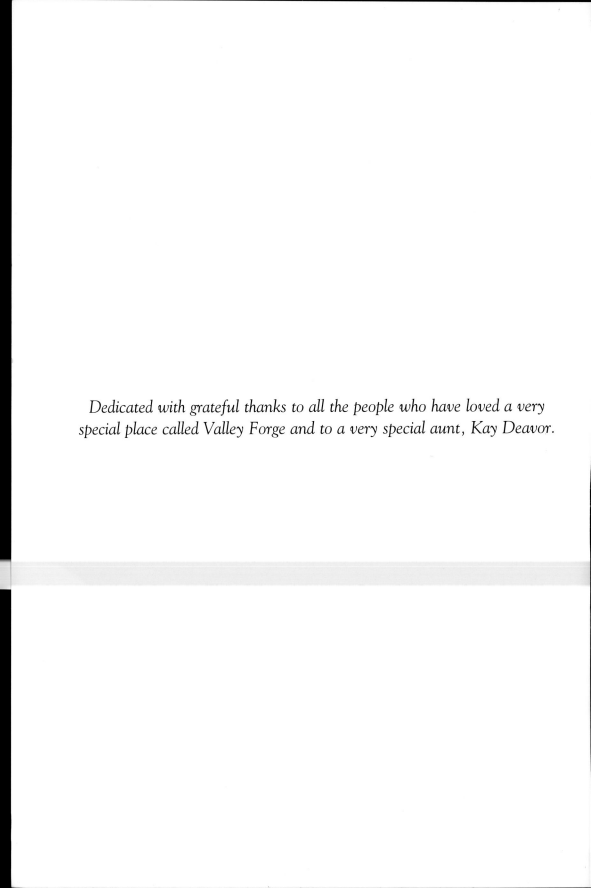

Dedicated with grateful thanks to all the people who have loved a very special place called Valley Forge and to a very special aunt, Kay Deavor.

IMAGES
of America

VALLEY FORGE

Stacey A. Swigart

ARCADIA

Copyright © 2002 by The Valley Forge Historical Society
ISBN 978-0-7385-1117-7

Published by Arcadia Publishing
Charleston SC, Chicago IL, Portsmouth NH, San Francisco CA

Printed in the United States of America

Library of Congress Catalog Card Number: 2002109278

For all general information contact Arcadia Publishing at:
Telephone 843-853-2070
Fax 843-853-0044
E-mail sales@arcadiapublishing.com
For customer service and orders:
Toll-Free 1-888-313-2665

Visit us on the Internet at www.arcadiapublishing.com

Contents

ACKNOWLEDGMENTS

Many people have played an important part in the history of Valley Forge, and many of them have touched my life directly and indirectly. While the names are too numerous to mention, I would like to express special thanks to the following: W. Herbert Burk; Eleanor Stroud Burk; Frances Liggett; Ruby Bloomer and "Chopper;" Margaret Conner; L. Davis Jones; Meade B. Jones; Edward W. Richardson; Herman O. Benninghoff II; Molly Swigart; Matt Swigart; my family; the "Team"—Joan Benninghoff, Marc Brier, Dona McDermott, and Michelle Ortwein; and the "Girls"—Nancy Dogan, Beverly Perry, Kathy Roscoe, MaryAnne Webster, and Audrey Wilkins.

INTRODUCTION

Valley Forge—just the name conjures images of soldiers, snow, and starvation. At the same time, however, Valley Forge has come to mean victory, triumph over despair, and most of all a monument to the founding of the United States of America.

In 1777, Gen. George Washington was trying to protect the city of Philadelphia, the home of Continental Congress. The British, in turn, were seeking to capture the city, feeling that if the "capital" of the country fell into their hands, they could swiftly end the war. After a variety of skirmishing and battles at Brandywine and Germantown, the British entered the city. The Continental Congress had evacuated to York, Pennsylvania, some 90 miles west of Philadelphia. Valley Forge was chosen because of the defensible ground, the proximity to Philadelphia, and its location as middle ground between Congress and the occupied city. Washington could protect Congress and keep an eye on the activities of the British in Philadelphia.

More than 15,000 men, women, and children encamped at Valley Forge for six months. They were from various backgrounds, ethnic groups, nationalities, and religions. All 13 colonies were represented at Valley Forge by either individuals or troops. The Continental army was reorganized and retrained under the direction of Baron von Steuben. The alliance with France was announced at Valley Forge, providing much needed moral support and funds. With the departure of the British from Philadelphia on June 18, 1778, the Continental army evacuated Valley Forge a day later in pursuit. The two armies would clash at Monmouth, New Jersey, with American success. The training had worked.

After the Continental army marched out of Valley Forge in 1778, the lands returned to farming and industry, and the inhabitants began building their lives once the war was finally over. During the Constitutional Convention of 1787, George Washington supposedly rode out on horseback from Philadelphia to visit the grounds where he and his men had spent the winter. He might have been the first official visitor to go to Valley Forge to remember and commemorate the events, struggles, and triumphs that took place there.

Efforts to save George Washington's home, Mount Vernon, in Virginia were under way as early as 1853. By the time of the centennial in 1876, there was a resurgence of patriotic fervor. In the same manner that women gathered to save Mount Vernon, a group of interested citizens gathered at Valley Forge to save Washington's Headquarters. By the turn of the century, interest in historical subjects was important to people around the world.

After a visit to Valley Forge and finding no answers to some of his questions, Dr. Rev. W. Herbert Burk, an Episcopal minister, began seeking a way to commemorate the events and honor the people who served there. His plan was the Washington Memorial—a wayside chapel to serve the spiritual needs of people from around the nation who came to Valley Forge and a museum dedicated to the history of America. The Washington Memorial in Valley Forge was founded at a time in which Revolutionary War sites were invested with a spiritual significance and their importance and symbolic role were acknowledged through the establishment of memorials, patriotic associations, and other testimonials.

This book is only a portion of the story of Valley Forge, focusing primarily on the events of the early to mid-20th century. Many events have occurred in the Washington Memorial at Valley Forge since its founding. All of the stories of Valley Forge cannot be told here; it would encompass several volumes. However, the rich visual history is shared here in a way it has never been shared before. For an in-depth history of Valley Forge after the Revolutionary War encampment, the best source is the 1995 book of Lorett Treese, *Valley Forge: Making and Remaking a National Symbol* (see bibliography). It is a wonderful account of the organizations, people, and efforts to save the history of Valley Forge.

Images are from the collection of the National Center for the American Revolution and the Valley Forge Historical Society.

One

VALLEY FORGE

On December 19, 1777, the Continental army marched into Valley Forge after a difficult campaign in and around the Philadelphia region. Immediately upon arrival, they began constructing the huts they would live in for the next six months. The army was not in good shape. The campaign had been hard, and morale was low from several defeats. On December 23, George Washington wrote to the president of Congress, "I am now convinced, beyond a doubt that unless some great and capital change suddenly takes place . . . this Army must inevitably be reduced to one or other of these three things. Starve, dissolve, or disperse."

Prior to the events that made Valley Forge so famous, the forge that gave Valley Forge part of its name was an important early industry to the area. It required waterpower, and the Valley Creek (a tributary of the Schuylkill River) provided it. Today, its meandering path marks the location of the boundaries between Chester and Montgomery Counties.

THE VALLEY FORGE. Images of the Valley Forge are virtually nonexistent. An artist by the name of Strickland rendered an image in the 19th century upon which this original pen and ink was based. Henry T. MacNeill, a local artist, completed this image in 1957.

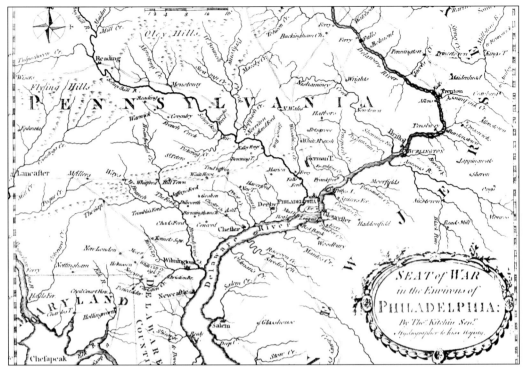

THE SEAT OF WAR, 1777. This map, entitled "Seat of War in the Environs of Philadelphia," was drawn by Thomas Kitchin Sr., hydrographer to the king of England. Originally published for the *London Magazine* in 1777, the map highlights roads, villages, creeks, and rivers in the region of Philadelphia (including New Jersey and Maryland).

WASHINGTON AND LAFAYETTE AT VALLEY FORGE. This engraving, by 19th-century artist Alonzo Chappel, depicts Gen. George Washington and the Marquis de Lafayette visiting the soldiers at Valley Forge. The Marquis was only 19 years old when he arrived in the United States. Washington never had children of his own, and the two men bonded together in their military service like father and son.

MARTHA WASHINGTON AT VALLEY FORGE. A 19th-century depiction of the camp by H.G. Ferris includes Martha Washington visiting the troops. Martha arrived in February 1778 to be with her husband.

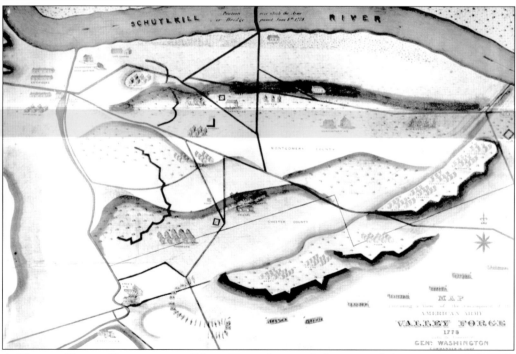

A VALLEY FORGE ENCAMPMENT MAP. Created around the time of the centennial (1876), this map identifies the various structures used by the officers of the Continental army and the locations of brigades. The map was created by David G. Smith after verbal descriptions from William Dewees, who served as a colonel and was present during the encampment at Valley Forge.

A VIEW OF VALLEY CREEK. This image provides a good view of why Valley Creek was so named. The creek is situated in a valley between two large hills, Mount Joy to the east and Mount Misery to the west.

A VIEW OF VALLEY CREEK. This picturesque view of Valley Creek shows some ducks near the water's edge, as well as a grazing sheep. Sadly, this photograph also shows some trash that has been dumped near the creek bed.

BOATS ON VALLEY CREEK. Up until 1920, there was a dam near the Washington's Headquarters building. Early-20th-century visitors to Valley Forge were able to rent small boats and enjoy the water. The dam was destroyed by order of the Valley Forge Park Commission in order to restore the area to the time of the winter encampment of 1777–1778.

THE FORGE AT VALLEY FORGE. Various studies, reports, and archeological research have been undertaken to discover the locations and construction dates of the various forges and buildings constructed at Valley Forge. This *c.* 1915 image depicts an alleged forge site along Valley Creek.

A VIEW OF VALLEY CREEK. This photograph of Valley Creek with a light dusting of snow on the ground was taken from the north. During the encampment, the soldiers reported some difficulty in accessing the water in the creek and the river to the height of the slopes along the bank.

Two

VALLEY FORGE PARK

After the Continental army left Valley Forge in 1778, the former encampment grounds reverted back to farmland. A rebirth of patriotic fervor grew around the centennial. By 1877, a group at Valley Forge was formed to commemorate the 100th anniversary of the Valley Forge encampment. It was called the Centennial and Memorial Association. In 1878, they reorganized in efforts to purchase the former headquarters building of Gen. George Washington. Their first regent was Anna Morris Holstein. After a number of years and donations from a variety of sources, including the Patriotic Order Sons of America, Washington's Headquarters was saved.

Valley Forge State Park was the first state park in Pennsylvania. It was established in 1893. Under the administration of the Valley Forge Park Commission, the park grew and expanded its boundaries. The park was transferred through federal legislation to operate under the direction of the National Park Service during the bicentennial in 1976. Pres. Gerald R. Ford signed the bill in 1976 at Valley Forge, and Valley Forge National Historical Park was born.

WASHINGTON'S HEADQUARTERS. This photograph shows Washington's Headquarters as seen from the west side of Valley Creek. In the distance are the Valley Forge train station platform and the small bridge over Valley Creek. Valley Creek feeds into the Schuylkill River.

15

THE ISAAC POTTS HOUSE. Gen. George Washington started living at Valley Forge in his campaign tents. He soon moved into the Isaac Potts house, renting it from Deborah Hewes. Over the years, much research and many renovations have taken place. Under various terms of leadership in the park commission, picket and stone fencing was added, removed, and added again. Artillery would often be seen on the lawn in front of headquarters, such as small and large cannon and cannonballs, regardless of historical accuracy.

WASHINGTON'S HEADQUARTERS. This picturesque rendering of Washington's Headquarters appeared on an early-20th-century postcard. Souvenirs and pictures of Washington's Headquarters and other monuments, as well as views of Valley Forge, were very popular with tourists who visited the region.

WASHINGTON'S HEADQUARTERS, A SIDE VIEW. This photograph shows the south side of Washington's Headquarters. To the right is the small log dining addition that was added in the 19th century to replicate the one used by Washington during the encampment. The kitchen addition was removed sometime in the mid-1920s.

WASHINGTON'S HEADQUARTERS. Pictured is the exterior of Washington's Headquarters in the early 20th century. In the 19th century, rumors began that secret escape routes were made for Washington in case of a surprise attack by the British. Secret doors, escape tunnels, and the like were all mentioned as part of the building. The escape tunnel was said to have a path to the Schuylkill River, where Washington could flee by boat. These rumors, however, have never been substantiated.

WASHINGTON'S HEADQUARTERS. The two-story, three-bay stone home was probably built in the late 1760s or early 1770s, possibly as a summer home for the Potts family. The small kitchen wing probably postdates the original structure after the Revolution. Over the years, a variety of restorations have taken place at headquarters, including the removal, replacement, and removal again of a second story over the kitchen wing.

WASHINGTON'S HEADQUARTERS. Valley Forge was increasingly becoming an important destination spot for tourists in the 19th century. The centennial of the nation and the World's Fair in Philadelphia in 1876 all brought increased visitation. Under the leadership of the Centennial and Memorial Association, Washington's Headquarters was open to the public for tours.

WASHINGTON'S HEADQUARTERS, INTERIOR. In the early 20th century, the Valley Forge Chapter of the Daughters of the American Revolution requested permission to furnish Washington's bedroom in the Potts house, as seen here. Furnishings were gathered to reflect the time period and were not necessarily accurate to Washington's stay in the house. Evidently, the

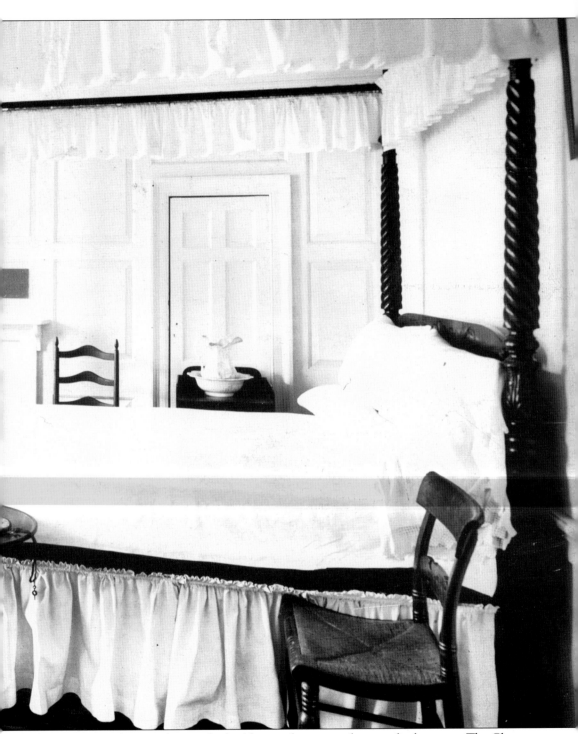

bedposts were too large to fit into the building and were cut down to fit the space. The Chester County Chapter of the Daughters of the American Revolution decorated another, a room with a round window considered Washington's "observatory."

WASHINGTON'S HEADQUARTERS. Over the years, many changes have taken place in the structure of the Isaac Potts house. The breezeway has been opened and closed several times, and a variety of outlying buildings from the 19th century were removed.

WASHINGTON'S HEADQUARTERS. This photograph shows the east (rear) side of headquarters with the kitchen addition still attached. Early visitors could tour the house and the kitchen addition and could visit a dark dirt cellar, which helped feed fuel to the rumor of a secret passageway in the building. Evidence suggests that the cellar was just that—a root cellar built by the family in residence in the 1840s.

THE WASHINGTON'S HEADQUARTERS ENTRANCE HALL. The Centennial and Memorial Association acquired the earliest furnishings for headquarters by donation and purchase after the building opened to the public. Objects were acquired for style and not for accuracy.

THE WASHINGTON'S HEADQUARTERS OFFICE. This is an early image of the office where Washington and his aides-de-camp would prepare and respond to correspondence. Some rooms were furnished somewhat informally to give the visitor the idea that Washington may have just left on important business.

WASHINGTON'S HEADQUARTERS. The oldest known photograph in existence of Washington's Headquarters, this 1861 image shows the kitchen addition stuccoed over and the breezeway

covered. A wooden lean-to structure is attached to the kitchen. At the time of this photograph, the Potts house was a residence under private ownership.

THE OFFICERS HEADQUARTERS. During encampments in the American Revolution, generals were usually housed in the homes of local families to accommodate their activities and staff. Shown here are the former headquarters of the Marquis de Lafayette and William Alexander Stirling. Both buildings survive today and are under the management of the Valley Forge National Historical Park.

THE DAVID POTTS HOUSE. The David Potts House, or William Dewees House, has also been known as the "Bake House" because it was believed that the bake ovens for the encampment were located here. During the 19th century, the structure was "victorianized" with wrought-iron balconies and a fancy cupola and became known as the Washington Inn.

THE DAVID POTTS HOUSE. The "Bake House" probably did not have the large-scale baking ovens that early historians thought. The Washington Inn was a hotel and restaurant operation that eventually closed after the park commission bought the building in the 1930s.

VARNUM'S HEADQUARTERS. This building was purchased by the park commission in 1918. Built in the first quarter of the 18th century, it is one of the oldest buildings in Valley Forge. Renovations were funded with support of the Philadelphia Chapter of the Daughters of the American Revolution.

MAXWELL'S QUARTERS. Also known as Valley Forge Farm, this historic house (a portion) served as the headquarters of Brig. Gen. William Maxwell. Additions were added over time. The farm was once the home of early-20th-century Attorney General Philander Chase Knox.

THE NATIONAL MEMORIAL ARCH DEDICATION. The dedication ceremony for the arch took place on June 19, 1917. The event was attended by several hundred visitors and a number of U.S. congressmen. Martin Brumbaugh, the governor of Pennsylvania, delivered the keynote speech.

THE DESIGN DRAWING FOR ARCH. Originally, there were plans for two arches at Valley Forge—one dedicated to George Washington and one to Baron von Steuben—at each entrance to the park. A single arch, a federally funded project, was approved by Congress in 1910. The arch was designed by Paul Philippe Cret, a professor at the University of Pennsylvania.

THE NATIONAL MEMORIAL ARCH. This view of the arch was taken sometime around the time of its completion in 1914, and its dedication was in June 1917. The design was inspired by the Arch of Titus in Rome. From its beginning construction, there was some controversy over the choice of a triumphal arch in a rural landscape; historically, arches were placed in urban areas. The project cost $100,000 to build, and an additional $35,000 was spent on topographical improvements.

THE MEMORIAL ARCH. In this image, a young visitor stands under the arch, reading the inscription of 19th-century orator Henry Armitt Brown. On the opposite wall (unseen) is a list of the officers who served at Valley Forge. The south elevation has a famous quotation from George Washington: "Naked and starving as they are we cannot enough admire incomparable patience and fidelity of the soldiery," from a letter to New York Gov. George Clinton on February 16, 1778.

THE SULLIVAN BRIDGE MARKER. On December 22, 1777, it was announced to the Continental army that Maj. Gen. John Sullivan had undertaken the direction of a bridge to be built across the Schuylkill River from the main encampment grounds to the north side of the river. Washington excused Sullivan from "common duties of the camp" in order to expedite its construction. The first marker in Valley Forge to commemorate a portion of the encampment was one for Sullivan's bridge in the mid-19th century.

THE SCHUYLKILL RIVER. This view of the Schuylkill River was taken from the south side of the river, looking north. In his Valley Forge guidebook, W. Herbert Burk identifies the spot as "Fatland Ford," the spot where the British crossed the Schuylkill River in September 1777.

THE "WATERMAN" MONUMENT. This stone marker was originally dedicated in 1901 by the Daughters of the American Revolution of 1776. It stands 50 feet high and is 10 feet wide at its base. The marker is dedicated to all the soldiers who lost their lives at Valley Forge, but it is more commonly known as the Waterman Monument due to its location near the only known grave marker of John Waterman.

THE WATERMAN MARKER. The only gravestone at Valley Forge was located on the grand parade ground. Simply marked on the stone is "JW 1778." The stone was located near the area where Rhode Island regiments encamped while at Valley Forge. "JW" was later identified as John Waterman in a letter at the Rhode Island Historical Society. Over the years, people began chipping away at the stone for souvenirs. Since the gravestone was located on private property, the Sons of the American Revolution sought and obtained permission from the owner to surround the stone with a chain-link fence to protect it from further damage. Today, the stone is in the collection of the Valley Forge National Historical Park.

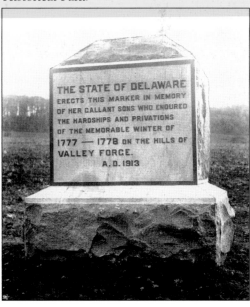

THE DELAWARE MARKER. The monument for the patriots from the state of Delaware was dedicated in 1914. There was only one Delaware regiment, and it actually did not spend the winter at Valley Forge. Capt. Allen McLane of Delaware and his regiment did spend the winter at Valley Forge, successfully harassing British foraging parties and keeping Washington informed of British movements in the region.

THE KNOX BRIDGE. Originally built in 1865, the covered bridge spans across Valley Creek. It was named for former Attorney General Philander Chase Knox, whose farm was nearby. Today, it is a popular site for local artists to render the image in paintings and photographs.

THE RUINS AT VALLEY FORGE. Ruins of 19th-century industrial buildings and tenant worker's homes at Valley Forge were still surviving in the early 20th century. When the park commission began managing the park, plans were made to restore Valley Forge to its 1777–1778 views.

INDUSTRY AT VALLEY FORGE. After the forge was destroyed by the British in 1777 and the Continental army left Valley Forge in 1778, the industries of Valley Forge started to grow again. A major business was a textile mill, seen here with a goat in the foreground. Other businesses included a saw factory, wrought iron (until *c.* 1816), and a lime quarry with kilns to burn lime.

A HUT RUIN AT VALLEY FORGE. W. Herbert Burk often told the story of how he heard that an original hut was still in existence on one of the farms in Valley Forge. With camera in hand, he went to document the hut but found that a farmer was dismantling it. This hut is purported to be the last of the huts at Valley Forge.

THE OBSERVATORY TOWER. The observatory at Valley Forge was built in the 1920s by the park commission. In the 1928 edition of *Historical and Topographical Guide to Valley Forge*, W. Herbert Burk states, "The Park Commission has won the gratitude of visitors to Valley Forge by the erection of the Mount Joy Observatory, whose platform is 500 feet above the sea level. From this vantage point there is a magnificent view of the surrounding country. To aid visitors to the appreciation of the strategic value of the site selected by Washington and his generals, a cast-iron plate has been placed on the platform, giving the direction and distance of each important place in the vicinity of Valley Forge." Unfortunately, due to the age of the tower and the expense of upkeep, not to mention the liabilities of such a structure, the tower was torn down in the 1980s.

THE OLD SCHOOLHOUSE. For many years, this building was thought to have been an 18th-century schoolhouse that was used as a hospital during the encampment. Early in the history of the park, it was interpreted as such. However, recent research has led experts to believe the structure was built after 1790. This was the second historic building acquired by the state park.

THE OLD SCHOOLHOUSE, INTERIOR. The schoolhouse opened to the public on May 15, 1908, with an interior setting of an early school complete with desks, benches, and a teacher's desk. The park commission wrote after the opening that they "have been placed in their proper positions, and thus the young of the present have an object lesson as to the manner with which the inculcation of the youth with the rudiments of education was imparted in earlier days."

THE HOSPITAL HUT. A reproduction hospital hut was constructed purportedly on the site of an original hospital hut. The design was based on a description in a poem by Albigence Waldo, a camp surgeon at Valley Forge. It is not known whether he was the true author, or if the poem was from the era of the encampment.

THE HOSPITAL HUT, INTERIOR. The interior of the hospital hut features a number of beds with "ticking" mattresses, pillows, and blankets. Dried herbs hang from the ceiling. In reality, the beds would have been covered with straw that hopefully would have been changed with each patient.

SOLDIERS AT THE WAYNE STATUE. Valley Forge was a place for people of all ages, races, and backgrounds to come together. Boy Scouts held a number of "jamborees" in the park, and

soldiers would often visit the area before heading off to war. Here, soldiers congregate beneath the statue of Anthony Wayne.

THE ANTHONY WAYNE MONUMENT. The largest bronze statue in Valley Forge, commemorating Brig. Gen. "Mad" Anthony Wayne, began with a $30,000 appropriation from the Pennsylvania government. Henry K. Bush-Brown of Newburgh, New York, designed the statue. The dedication ceremony took place on June 19, 1908, with more than 3,000 people in attendance.

A MONUMENT TO THE UNKNOWN DEAD. This monument was dedicated on June 11, 1911. The Valley Forge Chapter of the Daughters of the American Revolution funded its construction. The park commission chose the location of the monument, a site where soldiers who died during the encampment may have been buried. During the encampment, more than 2,000 soldiers died, mostly from disease. This particular site is located on Mount Joy.

THE STAR REDOUBT. The Star Redoubt at Valley Forge, an earthwork defensive fortification, is shaped like its name. It was constructed in 1916. The original lines of the redoubt were visible as late as 1850.

THE STAR REDOUBT. This is a view of the Star Redoubt from the opposite direction. Many different types of fencing structures were erected in Valley Forge surrounding monuments, memorials, and constructions during the early part of the 20th century.

A MASSACHUSETTS MONUMENT. Sponsored by the Commonwealth of Massachusetts, this monument is located near the Memorial Arch. It was dedicated in 1911. A unique "interactive" monument in the park, the Massachusetts Monument invites a visitor to sit on its bench and enjoy the scenery.

A VIEW FROM FORT HUNTINGTON. This view is from the base of Mount Joy, looking east. In the distance is the Stephens Farm (General Varnum's headquarters during the encampment), and you can just see the Waterman Monument by its white shaft in the distance.

A VIEW ACROSS THE SCHUYLKILL RIVER. This is another view from Mount Joy, looking north. The smoke is from a train heading west through Valley Forge. The vistas from the high ground in Valley Forge show the strong defensible position Washington and his troops held during the encampment.

A VALLEY FORGE ROAD. Since the creation of the automobile, visitors have enjoyed traveling to Valley Forge in their cars. According to records in the Pennsylvania State Archives, park guards have been complaining about tourists and the speeds with which they drive through the park since 1908.

THE PENNSYLVANIA COLUMNS. The Pennsylvania Columns were constructed in stages. The columns were built c. 1908, and the eagles and bronze reliefs of Pennsylvania generals were added in 1910. Henry Bush-Brown of Newburgh, New York, was the artist.

A VIEW OF THE SCHUYLKILL RIVER. This view of the Schuylkill River shows the train tracks that run along its bank through Valley Forge. Passenger trains dropped off visitors at the Valley Forge station near Washington's Headquarters on a daily basis during the first half of the 20th century. By the 19th century, several railroad lines—including the Pennsylvania Central, the Reading, and the Northern Pennsylvania—serviced Valley Forge.

VALLEY CREEK. Valley Forge offered visitors in the 19th century wonderful views and natural resources. Today, visitors take advantage of the same views as well as wooded trails and paths, a bike path, and tours of historic resources.

A WINTER AT VALLEY FORGE. The encampment at Valley Forge is remembered mainly for its winter weather. Temperatures fluctuated frequently, and half the six months of the encampment were in the spring when warmer weather returned. W. Herbert Burk carried his camera around the countryside, even in the snow, to document the landscape of the area and to capture the winter feeling.

THE GULPH ROAD. At the top of Mount Joy, this boulevard winds down the slopes of the hill. In the 1920s and 1930s, the hillside was covered with dogwood trees and featured displays of artillery and cannonballs.

A ROAD IN VALLEY FORGE. One of the entrances to the park, this road leads to the Memorial Arch. To the right is a 12-mile-per-hour speed limit sign for cars in the park. W. Herbert Burk's *Historical and Topographical Guide to Valley Forge* highlighted the places to see in the Valley Forge area and included mileage distances to businesses in the area for motorists.

A View over Valley Creek. Valley Creek is seen from Inner Line Drive on Mount Joy. After the park commission made plans in 1920 to restore the creek, many structures—including unfinished trolley tracks and their piers, a dam, and a mill—were destroyed.

INNER LINE DRIVE. A scenic view from Mount Joy, this photograph was given to W. Herbert Burk for the museum as a gift from photographer F. Radel. Burk documented Valley Forge in photographs himself and hired professional photographers for documenting the construction and development of the Washington Memorial.

A ROAD IN VALLEY FORGE. The roads in Valley Forge were conceptualized in the late 1890s after the park commission complained to the government of Pennsylvania about paths being worn into original fortifications by visitors to the area. Inner Line Drive was created in 1904, and Outer Line Drive was created in 1906.

A SITE OF THE BAKE OVENS. An early-20th-century iron marker denotes the location of an early bake oven. More recently (1999–2001), camp cooking sites have been unearthed in recent excavations at the park.

THE GRAVE OF AN UNKNOWN SOLDIER. Today, many of the sites that have markers for graves or burial grounds are questioned by researchers. This particular site is located on Mount Joy.

Three

THE WASHINGTON MEMORIAL

On Washington's Birthday 1903, W. Herbert Burk preached a sermon at the Norristown All Saints Church, of which he was rector. From the sermon, an idea was formulated: the Washington Memorial. The idea behind the memorial had many facets. The two major themes were the chapel and the museum.

Milton B. Medary, of the Philadelphia architectural firm Medary, Zantzinger, and Borie, designed the Washington Memorial complex. Fundraising efforts were long and arduous. Although construction was begun in 1903, the building was not completed until 1917.

The Washington Memorial was never completed as originally conceived. Burk's ideas and the funding never seemed to coincide. Money would be raised, and construction would continue until the funds ran out. The walls of the chapel would be raised in stone to a certain level and then boarded over with wood for a roof until more stonework could be accomplished. Large portions of the funds for the building of the church were acquired through the fundraising efforts of the clergy staff at the Episcopal church in Philadelphia.

What is remarkable is that Burk accomplished so much in the 30 years he spent at Valley Forge. The money he raised went toward the construction of the chapel and the ancillary structures—the Valley Forge Museum and the Valley Forge Historical Society, including all the collections. The funds also supported Sunday schools, parish mission projects, the construction of a cemetery, and much more.

THE WASHINGTON MEMORIAL. This is an image of the Washington Memorial as complete with the sanctuary and museum.

W. Herbert Burk. W. Herbert Burk wore a variety of hats at the Washington Memorial. He served as the rector of the Washington Memorial Chapel; as the president and curator of the Valley Forge Historical Society; as a speaker on such topics as George Washington, Valley Forge, and religion; and as the author of a variety of books, including a Valley Forge guidebook, which was first published in 1906 and was updated continuously through 1932. His photographs of Valley Forge are featured prominently in the guide.

THE WASHINGTON MEMORIAL. The original plan of the Washington Memorial as dreamed by W. Herbert Burk was designed by Milton B. Medary, a Philadelphia architect. The library was originally proposed to be in the front of the structure, adjacent to the front of the chapel. For years, the drawing of the proposed memorial building was the masthead for stationery for the Washington Memorial.

A PATRIOTS HALL CERTIFICATE. Original donors to the Washington Memorial construction were given small tokens of appreciation for the donations such as buttons, pictures, poems, and certificates. This certificate was given to donors toward Patriots Hall, a lecture and meeting space in the memorial. Of notable interest is the name on the certificate, Eleanor Stroud. Eleanor Stroud eventually married W. Herbert Burk in a simple ceremony in the unfinished chapel structure.

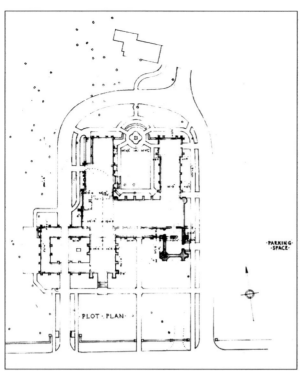

THE WASHINGTON MEMORIAL PLAN. The architectural plan for the Washington Memorial shows the layout of the property and conceived aspects for the building, including the Cloister of the Colonies, sanctuary, museum, library, bell tower, and gardens.

A WASHINGTON MEMORIAL MODEL. This model was commissioned by the Valley Forge Historical Society after new designs were drafted in the 1940s. The design is similar to W. Herbert Burk's original vision with the exception of his conceived library extension to the front of the bell tower.

56

THE WASHINGTON MEMORIAL.
Pictured are the architectural plans and a model view of the western side of the memorial. The images show the Cloister of the Colonies and the Open Air Cathedral.

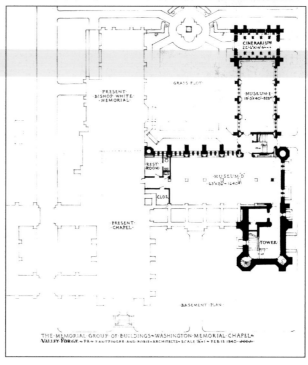

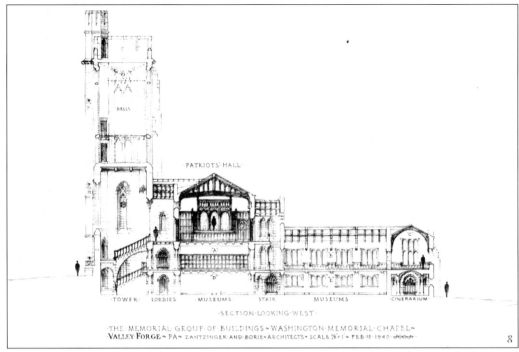

·BELLS·

·PATRIOTS'·HALL·

·A·

·D·

·TOWER· ·LOBBIES· ·MUSEUMS· ·STAIR· ·MUSEUMS· ·CINERARIUM·

·SECTION·LOOKING·WEST·

·THE·MEMORIAL·GROUP·OF·BUILDINGS~WASHINGTON·MEMORIAL·CHAPEL~
VALLEY·FORGE~PA~ ZANTZINGER·AND·BORIE~ARCHITECTS~SCALE ⅛″=1′~FEB·15·1940·   ·

8

THE WASHINGTON MEMORIAL. These views show a section of the architectural plans and a model view of the eastern side of the Washington Memorial. The areas shown here would include gallery space and meeting space in the museum.

Four

THE WASHINGTON MEMORIAL CHAPEL

The cornerstone for the Washington Memorial was laid on June 19, 1903. While the construction was beginning, a small barnboard structure was constructed to house the Valley Forge parishioners. It was at this wooden chapel (no longer in existence) in 1904 that Theodore Roosevelt became the first American president in office to visit Valley Forge.

On Washington's Birthday 1905, the first service was held in the partly built chapel. Rt. Rev. Robert Atkinson Gibson, bishop of Virginia, was a noted presence at the first service. His diocese (c. 1905) included the two parishes of which George Washington had been a vestryman.

THE WASHINGTON MEMORIAL CHAPEL. This is a very rare image of the chapel, including the original barnboard chapel that was constructed in 1903. Since its founding, the chapel has had five rectors: W. Herbert Burk, John Robbins Hart, Sheldon M. Smith, Richard Lyon Stinson, and R. James Larson.

W. HERBERT BURK. W. Herbert Burk, the son of an Episcopalian minister in New Jersey, was born in 1867. Before he was ordained in 1894, he received his bachelor's degree in divinity from the University of Pennsylvania and attended the Philadelphia Divinity School of the Protestant Episcopal Church. He served as rector to the Church of the Ascension in Gloucester City, New Jersey, St. John's in Norristown, Pennsylvania, and All Saints Church in Norristown. Burk died of a heart attack in 1933, and his remains were interred in the Washington Memorial Cemetery at his beloved Valley Forge.

THE CHAPEL, INTERIOR. These images show how the chapel was constructed in phases. The pulpit was finished in limestone, yet funds were needed for the floors, walls, and choir stalls. Temporary wooden walls were constructed as funds were raised.

THE CONSTRUCTION OF THE CHAPEL. This is a rare image of the memorial during construction. The view is from the western side near the museum entrance. The Porch of the Allies, yet to be

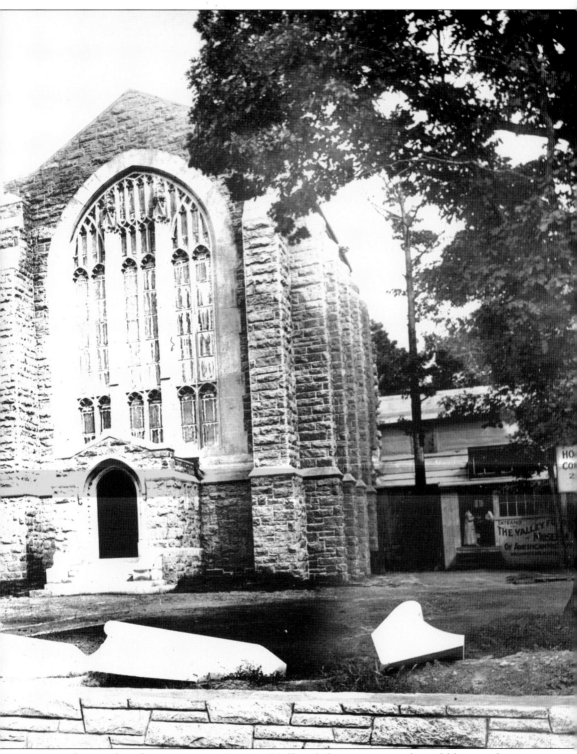

constructed, served as the entrance to Patriots Hall and the museum and would have a design that mimicked the architecture of the Cloister of the Colonies.

THE WASHINGTON MEMORIAL CHAPEL. This is a 1920s view of the chapel building.

FRIENDS OF VALLEY FORGE. People often gathered on the steps of the chapel for photographs. This group of dignitaries gathered in honor of the French Alliance of 1778 and the success of the Allies in World War I. The first row features, from left to right, Rev. James Henry Darlington, former president of the Huguenot Society; Gen. Robert George Nivelle, the hero of Verdun; and W. Herbert Burk.

A VIEW INTO THE CHAPEL. Taken in the Cloister of the Colonies, this image shows the view inside the sanctuary. There are two doors on the western side of the sanctuary, leading to the Cloister of the Colonies, and one on the western side, leading to the Porch of the Allies.

A VIEW OUT OF THE CHAPEL. Shown is a view similar to the previous photograph, except this viewpoint is from inside the chapel, looking out into the Cloister of the Colonies.

THE NEW JERSEY BAY, CLOISTER OF THE COLONIES. The New Jersey Bay was the first completed section of the Cloister of the Colonies. It is attached directly to the western side of the sanctuary.

THE UNFINISHED CLOISTER. This is a photograph of the construction of the cloister in progress. The construction took approximately 20 months to complete once the funds were raised.

THE CHAPEL ENTRANCE AND THE CLOISTER OF THE COLONIES. The front door was placed on the chapel porch at the top of the stone steps. Eventually, it was moved to the interior, and iron gates by ironmaster Samuel Yellin were placed at the immediate front entrance. The first two completed bays represent New Jersey and Pennsylvania.

THE CLOISTER OF THE COLONIES. The front bays of the cloister are complete here c. 1910. The chapel roof, visible at the top right, was constructed temporarily in wood due to a lack of funds to complete construction in stone.

THE CLOISTER OF THE COLONIES. Located to the west of the chapel, the cloister has 13 bays, each honoring one of the original colonies. The cloister forms a port cochere to the chapel. In this photograph, W. Herbert Burk stands near the cloister. Burk was dedicated to every aspect

of the memorial, the structure, the chapel, and the society. (Photograph by Henry R. Hippler, c. 1920.)

THE OPEN AIR CATHEDRAL. The western wall of the cloisters features the "Open Air Pulpit" in the New York Bay. W. Herbert Burk would refer to it as the "Open Air Cathedral" or "Woodland Pulpit" due to its location facing the woods next to the chapel. Crowds of some 15,000 people would sometimes congregate here for religious or patriotic ceremonies.

THE CLOISTER OF THE COLONIES. This view of the front of the Cloister of the Colonies is from the 1920s. Today, the chapel is a popular spot for weddings, and the cloister is sometimes used for special wedding photographs.

THE CLOISTER OF THE COLONIES FROM THE EAST. The Cloister of the Colonies is shown here from the Open Air Cathedral. At one time, W. Herbert Burk sought trees from Mount Vernon to plant here in the shape of a cross.

THE CHOIR DOOR. The doors in the Washington Memorial are made from richly carved oak. It was given in honor of Francis Hopkinson, poet and musician of the American Revolution. Adjacent in the same bay is the Door of the Allies, which opens into the New Hampshire Bay of the Cloister of the Colonies.

THE BELA PRATT STATUE. In the area surrounded by the Cloister of the Colonies, called the Garth, is a statue titled *Sacrifice and Devotion*, by Bela Pratt. The sculpture was given by a parishioner of the chapel in 1912 in honor of the mothers of the nation and as a memorial to his wife. It depicts a mother kneeling at an altar, holding in her hand the symbol of a mother's hope—a lighted lamp.

THE WASHINGTON MEMORIAL
DOOR. The front door to the chapel
was a gift of the Colonial Chapter
of the Daughters of the American
Revolution. It was dedicated on May
13, 1910. The door is located at
the entrance to the chapel, off the
porch, which was built with funds
from the All Saints Sunday School in
Norristown, Pennsylvania.

THE ROOF OF THE REPUBLIC. Filled with symbolism, the Roof of the Republic depicts the
carved and colored coat of arms of each state in the Union. Carved oak angels with outstretched
wings support the trusses of the roof, along with pelicans. The angels symbolize the providence
of God, and the pelicans symbolize self-sacrifice. Bronze plaques in the floor correlate to the
roof panels, identifying the names of the states.

PEW DESIGN. This is an original pen-and-ink wash of the design for the pews in the chapel. W. Herbert Burk wanted to replicate some of the designs of European gothic architecture. They are called the Pews of the Patriots and were designed by the architect of the building, Milton B. Medary Jr. At the base of each pew is carved the insignia of a patriotic society, a family coat of arms, or a state or Colonial seal.

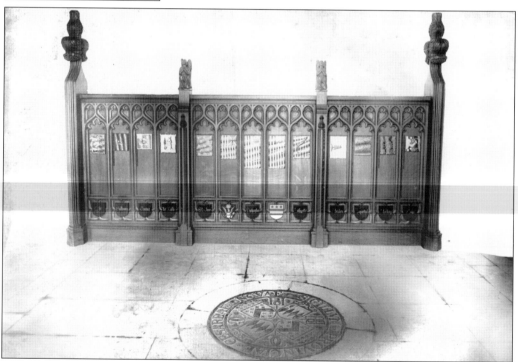

A PEW SCREEN. The screens in front of the first pews in the sanctuary commemorate the major generals and brigadier generals who served at Valley Forge. On this one, when artist G. Gerald Evans was finished, Burk had him deface the shield with Charles Lee's name on it (first one on the left). "Draw your chisel across it—the man was a traitor," he said, referring to Lee's retreat from the Battle at Monmouth, New Jersey, in 1778.

PEWS IN THE CHAPEL. The first pews were temporarily installed while there was still a wooden floor and the walls were unfinished (*c.* 1908–1910). Folding chairs are visible to the right, and the temporary wooden roof framing is visible at the top of the image.

PEWS AND FONT. Taken at the same time, this photograph shows the baptismal font to the right and an eerie double exposure of a gentleman standing to the right of the font. Carved from Indiana limestone, the font was named the Washington-Sullivan Font in commemoration of George Washington's baptism and in memory of the donor's son.

PEWS IN THE CHAPEL. Photographs of the construction of the chapel in progress are quite rare. Here are a couple of photographs of the pews in the sanctuary. W. Herbert Burk documented the progress of the construction work in photographs as his schedule allowed. As sections of the building and the furnishings were completed, new images would be taken to be included in the various editions of his book *Historical and Topographical Guide to Valley Forge*.

The Sanctuary of the Chapel. When the funds were finally acquired for the completion of the interior, the temporary pews and chairs were removed for the pouring of the floor and placement of the bronze plaques representing the states. This image was taken to document the space before everything was put in place. The "Life of Christ" window is above the altar.

WEST SIDE CHOIR STALL. The interior of the chapel was completed in phases just like the exterior walls and roof. Flags were to be placed over the woodwork of the choir stalls. Part of the original design of architect Milton B. Medary, they were carved by Philadelphia artist Edward Maene. The brigades who served at Valley Forge are commemorated in each stall, with wooden soldiers representing each brigade in the niches of the woodwork.

EAST SIDE CHOIR STALL. The soldiers carved into the woodwork were painted to reflect the regimental colors of their units from the 18th century. Also shown here is the lectern—the only portion of the chapel dedicated to a British officer, Gen. Edward Braddock. George Washington served under Braddock in the Seven Years' War, also known as the French and Indian War.

THE CLERGY SEATS. Carved stone "canopies" cover the sedilia, or clergy seats, next to the altar. They commemorate the rectors who served as ministers to George Washington. Related to the Episcopal church in Washington's era were Bishop White and Bishop Provoost.

THE CHAPEL, INTERIOR. Almost finished, the interior of the chapel is shown here *c.* 1930. On the stone altar is the altar cross of carved wood that is painted and gilded. The cross is dedicated to Abraham Lincoln, being a gift from "a Descendant of a Pennsylvania Ancestor of President Lincoln."

THE BISHOP WILLIAM WHITE LIBRARY, EXTERIOR. This library is dedicated to Bishop William White, chaplain of the Continental Congress as well as rector during George Washington's residence in Philadelphia as president. The memorial, including a bronze statue of the bishop in the garden behind the chapel, was a bequest of Harry Louis Peake.

THE BISHOP WILLIAM WHITE LIBRARY, INTERIOR. The library structure includes a fireplace, oak bookcases, and portraits of past rectors of the chapel. The library was originally designed to hold the Bishop William White Library of the chapel and the Washington Memorial Library of the Valley Forge Historical Society.

THE BISHOP WHITE LIBRARY, EXTERIOR. The main library entrance was on the western side of the building, next to the path leading up to the Cloister of the Colonies. A second door, which

exits into the garden on the opposite side of the library, was recently installed.

PEACE CHIME CARILLON. The Washington Memorial National Carillon began as the "Star-Spangled Banner National Peace Chime" of 13 bells representing the 13 original colonies on July 4, 1926. It was located in a structure to the west of the chapel until their removal and placement in the bell tower in 1958.

THE BELL TOWER, 1958. Funds for the construction of the bell tower were provided by the Daughters of the American Revolution. The tower was dedicated on April 15, 1958. The carillon holds 58 bells—28 cast by the Meneely Bell Foundry and 30 by Paccard of Annecy, France. Individually, the bells range in weight from 13.5 to 8,000 pounds.

A PENNSYLVANIA BELL. The bells
in the early carillon were cast
by the Meneely Bell Foundry of
Watervliet, New York.

THE UNVEILING OF A BELL. An
unidentified young woman and
W. Herbert Burk unveil a bell
for the Valley Forge carillon in a
ceremony *c.* 1930.

THE MARTHA WASHINGTON LOG CABIN. The cabin was constructed in 1915 by W. Herbert Burk and the boys of the Washington Memorial Chapel Sunday School. They hauled logs, placed them in position, and chinked the spaces between. Its first use was as a Sunday school building for the parish. During the winter of 1968–1969, the cabin was restored, and it is currently used as the Chapel Cabin Shop.

Five

THE VALLEY FORGE
HISTORICAL SOCIETY

W. Herbert Burk founded the Valley Forge Historical Society in 1918. In creating the Washington Memorial Chapel and the Valley Forge Historical Society, Burk recognized the twofold significance that Valley Forge had come to have for Americans. On the one hand, the memorial chapel paid tribute to the spiritual change in the Continental army that came out of the winter encampment of 1777–1778. The society, on the other hand, was devoted to collecting, preserving, and interpreting the material objects, documents, and records that were a part of the Valley Forge experience. In other words, the chapel recognized the symbolic and spiritual importance of Valley Forge, and the society and its programs were established to preserve and present the actual event of the Valley Forge encampment as well as other events of the Revolutionary War.

W. Herbert Burk began collecting for his original idea, the Valley Forge Museum of American History, in 1908. His plan was to have a "Smithsonian North" institution. He wanted a museum at Valley Forge dedicated to all eras of American history. The idea never came to fruition, but Burk continued to collect any and all material he could before his death in 1933. The collection he amassed was strong and important to American history. It is incredible to note that many items were purchased or gifted to the society during the years of the Great Depression. Burk never gave up; every nickel and dime counted for something.

THE ENTRANCE TO THE VALLEY FORGE MUSEUM. The former entrance to the Valley Forge Historical Society Museum is similar in design to the Cloister of the Colonies. Each bay in the Porch of the Allies is dedicated to a foreign general who served in the American Revolution—Johann DeKalb, Baron von Steuben, the Marquis de Lafayette, and the Count de Rochembeau.

THE MARQUEE. In 1907, W. Herbert Burk began a quest to acquire one of Gen. George Washington's war tents, his Marquee. At George Washington's death in 1799, the ownership of the tents reverted to his wife, Martha Washington. At her death in 1802, Martha's grandson George Washington Parke Custis acquired the tents and used them for special events and parties. The tents remained at his home Arlington, in Virginia, until his death. They were passed on to his daughter, who was married to Gen. Robert E. Lee. During the Civil War, the Custis-Lee family was forced from Arlington, and the property (including the tents) was seized by the federal government. After the close of the war, the Lee family petitioned the government for the return of their property. Mary Custis Lee (daughter to Robert E. Lee) offered the tents for sale at $5,000 each. Burk began a correspondence with Lee as she traveled the globe, negotiating the terms of the sale. W. Herbert Burk placed $500 down and agreed to make payments from the income of visitors viewing the exhibited tent at Valley Forge. Lee turned over all proceeds to her pet charity, the Old Confederate Women's Home in Richmond, Virginia. Upon its arrival at Valley Forge on August 20, 1909, W. Herbert Burk installed the tent in the museum.

THE MARQUEE EXHIBIT, C. 1950. The Marquee was never fully displayed at the Valley Forge Historical Society. The museum quarters were small, and the area would not accommodate the size of the full Marquee. Instead, the tent was displayed in a case with other memorabilia to a portion of its extended size, and the interior was used for storage space for the many artifacts that could not be displayed for lack of space.

THE SITE OF THE MARQUEE. On Inner Line Drive is the marker that denotes the traditional spot where Gen. George Washington pitched his tents when he moved into Valley Forge. He lived in his tents for approximately a week before moving into the Potts house. After bringing the original tent to Valley Forge, W. Herbert Burk greatly wanted to photograph the tent outside. A request to the Valley Forge Park Commission to set it up at the original (1777) location was denied. Burk instead chose to pitch the tent outside the Washington Memorial.

"No spot on earth—not the plains of Marathon, nor the passes of Sempach, nor the place of the Bastile, nor the dykes of Holland, nor the moors of England—is so sacred in the history of the struggles for human liberty as Valley Forge."—*Cyrus Townsend Brady.*

This is to certify that

a loyal American and a member of

in the State of   , having paid the annual dues of Ten Cents for one year, has been enrolled by the Valley Forge Historical Society a member of

The Valley Forge Legion
of the United States of America

Signed and Sealed at Valley Forge this   *day*

                    of   *, 193   , No.*

W. Herbert Burk

Founder and First President

Secretary

A VALLEY FORGE LEGION CERTIFICATE. Membership to the society in the late 1920s and early 1930s was available for a dues payment of 10¢. By 1932, the society boasted the largest membership of any historical organization for several years with over 67,000 members across the United States, many of them children. For 10¢, you would receive this certificate and a special button with the insignia of the Valley Forge Historical Society.

THE ENTRANCE TO THE MUSEUM. After a reorganization of the museum and the collections in 1950, the museum featured freshly painted walls, updated exhibits, and a group of volunteers who gave specially guided tours. A copy of the bronze bust by Jean-Antoine Houdon was prominently placed at the entrance to the galleries.

A Museum Exhibit. The museum went through a variety of changes over the years. In the 1950s, there was a significant cleanup and organization of the artifacts, and exhibits were changed or reinstalled with significant upgrades for the time period. The main gallery featured

changing exhibits. On view here are items from the china-porcelain collection; *The March to Valley Forge* painting, by William B.T. Trego; and, in the back, the painting *Washington before Trenton*, by John Trumbull.

A Museum Exhibit. In the 1950s, the society implemented a series of platform exhibits with items from the collection as well as objects borrowed from other institutions and individuals. These rotating exhibits allowed a wide variety of collections from storage to be seen by visitors and members on a regular basis.

A Museum Exhibit. Relying on a variety of loans from individuals and using items from the society collection, this platform exhibit featured doll furniture to complement prior exhibits on dolls and toys from American history.

A MUSEUM EXHIBIT. Furniture displays were popular subjects for the monthly platform exhibits in the museum. Members of the society, particularly members of the women's committee (auxiliary), loaned, labeled, and helped organize the various exhibits.

A MUSEUM EXHIBIT. Military exhibits from various eras of American military history were popular before the Valley Forge Historical Society decided to focus on the history of Valley Forge and the American Revolution exclusively. Here, the focus is the uniforms of the U.S. Army.

A MUSEUM EXHIBIT ROOM. This exhibit of Colonial-era household items was located below the main gallery space of the museum. Exhibits were rearranged, and a large variety of artifacts were displayed in relatively small settings on a rotating basis.

A MUSEUM EXHIBIT WITH GUIDE. In the 1950s and 1960s, visitors to the museum would receive guided tours for their nominal admission price. The volunteer guides would often dress in costume. While not historically accurate, they added atmosphere to the various displays.

A HOME DECORATIVE ARTS GALLERY. After the renovations of 1950, the volunteer curator at the time, Lloyd Eastwood-Siebold, designed a series of "Home and Decorative Arts Galleries." They featured the decorative arts collection of the society in homey settings, as seen here.

THE VALLEY FORGE MUSEUM OF AMERICAN HISTORY
THE WASHINGTON MEMORIAL LIBRARY
VALLEY FORGE

Valley Forge   19

Dear

The Committee on Library has received from you the following contribution to its collection

for which it returns its grateful acknowledgment

Librarian

To

THE WASHINGTON MEMORIAL LIBRARY CERTIFICATE. Gifts to the Washington Memorial Library for the Museum of American History were acknowledged with a certificate like this, designed by W. Herbert Burk. His desire was to replicate George Washington's library at Mount Vernon. His idea was never completed; however, he did build the foundation for a library that holds over 3,000 volumes of history on the Revolutionary War.

A George Washington Statue. W. Herbert Burk raised funds for a copy to be made of the full-length statue of George Washington by Jean-Antoine Houdon. The molds were lent by Gov. John G. Pollard of Virginia from the original made for the Virginia State House in Richmond. Originally displayed on the grounds near the Washington Memorial, it was moved next to Washington's Headquarters. It is now in the collection of Valley Forge National Historical Park.

BOY SCOUTS AT VALLEY FORGE. Boy Scouts and Girl Scouts were frequent visitors to Valley Forge and the museum. Children paid a large part in the development of the museum by becoming junior members of the society, helping to raise funds for artifacts or even donating objects. In this image, W. Herbert Burk accepts the donation of a stone bowl from a local chapter of Boy Scouts.

FRIENDS OF VALLEY FORGE. W. Herbert Burk had a large network of friends, parishioners, volunteers, and supporters. Here, a group stands in front of the entrance to the Valley Forge Museum of American History with Burk. From left to right are John Wanamaker (founder of John Wanamaker's, a Philadelphia department store), ? Stoudt, W. Herbert Burk, Harry E. Stinson, and Alfred H. Read.

MUSEUM STAFF. Throughout the existence of the Washington Memorial, there has always been a dedicated group of staff and volunteers. Pictured, from left to right, are Lloyd Eastwood-Siebold, curator of the Valley Forge Historical Society Museum; Rev. John Robbins Hart, rector of the chapel and president of the society; and Frances Liggett (seated), chairwoman of the women's committee for the society who led efforts with Siebold to reorganize the museum. All were members of the society and chapel. Past presidents of the society include W. Herbert Burk, John Robbins Hart, Mrs. Franklin B. Wildman, Howard W. Gross, L. Davis Jones, Meade B. Jones, Jean-Pierre Bouvel, and Adm. Thomas W. Lynch.

THE MARCH TO VALLEY FORGE. William B.T. Trego (Bucks County, Pennsylvania) created this oil painting in 1883 for a contest with the Pennsylvania Academy of Fine Arts. Trego won first prize, but the grand prize was not awarded to anyone, probably due to a lack of participation.

Trego went to court to try and obtain the monetary award that was given as the grand prize and lost. The painting was acquired by the Valley Forge Historical Society in 1930. It is purported that the image of the soldier saluting Washington is a self-portrait of the artist.

A Sculpture of George Washington. Sculpted by Franklin Simmons, this bronze was gifted to the society in 1930. It depicts George Washington after learning of the "Conway Cabal," an attempt to usurp his position as commander in chief of the Continental army. A companion piece was given to the Washington Memorial Chapel in 1908 by W. Herbert Burk in memory of his first wife. It sits in a niche near the choir stalls in the chapel.

GEORGE WASHINGTON'S BREECHES. Among the many items associated with George Washington at Valley Forge is a pair of breeches worn by him when he was president of the United States. Several years after acquiring the breeches, the society received a matching vest.

A TELESCOPE. Shown in a photograph taken by W. Herbert Burk, this telescope was given to George Washington by the Comte de Grasse, a French officer who supported the American cause during the Revolutionary War. It was made in France and is complete with its original tripod stand and wooden travel case.

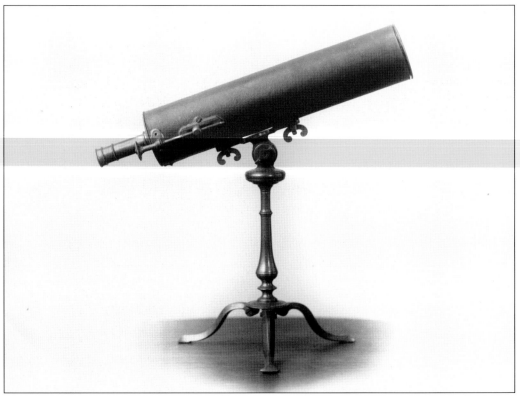

GEORGE WASHINGTON CAMP CUPS. In 1924, W. Herbert Burk acquired two silver camp cups of George Washington. They were originally from a set of 12, commissioned by Washington from Philadelphia silversmith Edmund Milne in August 1777. The other 10 were given to the society in a bequest by John Dobson in 1980.

THE "GWC" TEA SET. The Chinese export porcelain set shown here was commissioned by George Washington for his namesake, George Washington Craik. Craik was the son of Washington's physician, James Craik. It features the emblem of the masons, since both were members. The set was gifted to the society in the 1950s.

A Muster Roll of the Field & Staff Officers in the 4th Massachusetts Bay Regt commanded by Colonel Edward Wigglesworth taken for April 1778.

Names	Rank	Remarks
Edwd Wigglesworth	Colonel	on Command.
Dudley Colman	Lt Col:	
John Porter	Major	
John K. Smith	Adjt	
Wm Wigglesworth	Q Mar	
Ivory Hovey	Surgeon	on furlow
Thos Smart	Pay Mr	
Joseph Miller	Serj Maj	
James Green	Drm Maj:	
Elihu Spelman	D Maj:	
J. S. Holland	F. Maj:	on furlow

Camp Valley Forge
May 2d 1778 Then Mustered the Field & Staff Officers in Col: Wigglesworths Regt as specified in above Roll.

THE VALLEY FORGE MUSTER ROLL. Among the artifacts of the Valley Forge Historical Society are a number of historic documents. This document is a muster roll from the 4th Massachusetts Regiment under the command of Col. Edward Wigglesworth in April 1778 at Valley Forge.

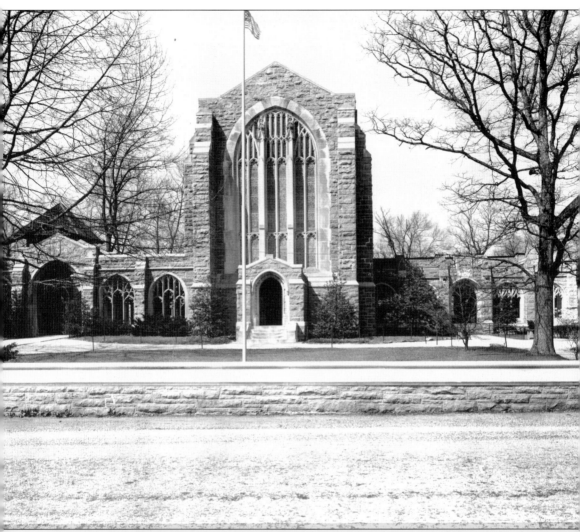

THE WASHINGTON MEMORIAL CHAPEL AND MUSEUM. Very few photographs of the original museum exist. Up until the late 1940s, the museum was still called the Valley Forge Museum of American History. In this image, a sign for the museum can be seen to the right of the museum entrance.

A GEORGE WASHINGTON PORTRAIT. One of the first paintings to be acquired for the museum by W. Herbert Burk was a portrait of George Washington. It was a gift of early-20th-century philanthropist J. Ackerman Coles. The portrait is said to have been rendered by the artist Gilbert Stuart, but experts and curators have agreed that it was completed by an unknown artist after a similar painting by Gilbert Stuart. It was originally owned by Washington Irving, the author of *The Legend of Sleepy Hollow*.

A CHINA COLLECTION. In the 1920s, W. Herbert Burk was fortunate to acquire the Thomas H. Schollenberger Memorial China Collection for the museum. The collection included some 4,000 pieces of all types of china and porcelain, including Staffordshire, Gaudy Welsh, and Gaudy Dutch wares, as well as pink, copper, and silver lusterwares. Burk and his wife transported the collection in their "Ford touring car" over a period of several weeks, packing and transporting the precious material from Pottsville, Pennsylvania, to Valley Forge. Some parishioners and clergy staff assisted in the move as they could. Burk reported only one broken plate.

BLUE STAFFORDSHIRE. In the 1950s and 1960s, the china collections, particularly the Blue Staffordshire, were displayed in several rooms that now serve the chapel as Sunday school rooms. Both the society and the chapel would hold a variety of events and receptions surrounded by fine china wares, such as "State Sunday Service Teas" and "Lunch Lectures with the Curator."

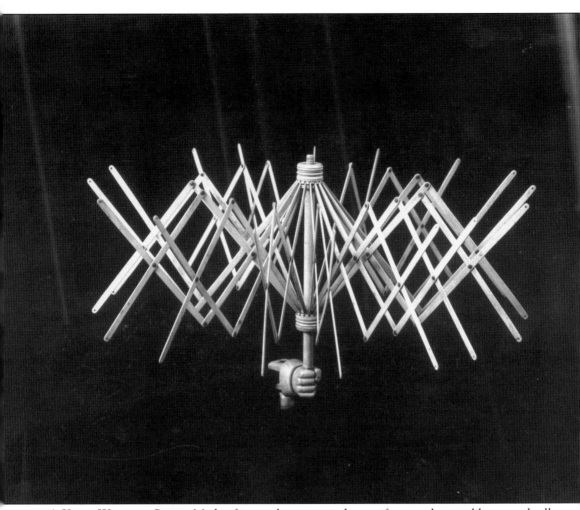

A YARN-WINDING SWIFT. Made of ivory, the yarn-winding swift expands open like an umbrella. This photograph was taken by W. Herbert Burk soon after acquiring the piece from the Washington family in the 1920s. The swift is purported to have belonged to Martha Washington.

THE HANGING ROCK. Before arriving in Valley Forge on December 19, 1777, the Continental army encamped briefly in Gulph Mills, several miles east of Valley Forge. Legends have persisted for well over 100 years about how George Washington and his army traveled under this "overhanging rock" on their way to Valley Forge. Since the inception of the car, the state department of transportation has tried to remove the rock. The first "rally" around the rock came in 1924, when it was given to the society. After public outcry over the years, the rock was placed on the National Register of Historic Places in 1997.

THE PRESENTATION OF THE HANGING ROCK. An unidentified girl unveils the memorial plaque placed on the Hanging Rock in a ceremony in 1924. Visitors could travel to Gulph Mills by train and visit the site of the rock, which at one time had several levels of stairs and decks that could be climbed to the peak.

A GEORGE WASHINGTON PLAY. Among W. Herbert Burk's many talents was writing. He authored a number of books, wrote a variety of sermons and lectures, and even tried his hand at writing plays. Usually focusing on one of his favorite subjects, George Washington, he wrote a play that was eventually performed at a local high school in Norristown, Pennsylvania.

A George Washington Play. In scenes from his play of George Washington, unidentified actors share scenes on stage. It is assumed that the scene with the ladies on stage represents Martha Washington and the women of Valley Forge gathering to sew for the soldiers.

A GEORGE WASHINGTON PLAY. They "boys" of the army and the entire cast gather on stage with their muskets in these photographs. W. Herbert Burk loved children. The whole idea for the Washington Memorial—chapel and museum—started with a trip to Valley Forge by Burk and the boys' choir of All Saints Church. When the boys began asking questions about the history of the encampment, Burk could not answer, so he set about to create a place to learn and memorialize.

A GEORGE WASHINGTON PLAY. The adults of the play gather on stage for a curtain call, and a number of girls share a scene, possibly to sing "The Star-Spangled Banner." Events such as plays, teas, luncheons, and garden parties were held on a regular basis to help with fundraising efforts for the society. Funds were needed for construction, acquiring artifacts and operating the museum.

ARMY MILITARY STREAMERS. In the 1950s, the Valley Forge Historical Society was honored to be the only private institution gifted with a set of the U.S. Army Battle Streamers—representing every battle fought by the U.S. Army since its founding in 1775. In 1993, through the efforts of Rep. Curt Weldon of Pennsylvania, the streamers for the Gulf War were added to the collection.

Six

THE FUTURE OF VALLEY FORGE

The Valley Forge of today is in the midst of great changes. In 1999, federal legislation authorized a partnership between Valley Forge National Historical Park and the Valley Forge Historical Society to create a new museum dedicated to the entire history of the Revolutionary War. In 2000, the National Center for the American Revolution was created to lead the campaign. The Valley Forge Historical Society no longer operates a museum in the Washington Memorial building; it closed its doors on February 1, 2002. The history of the society and the collection will live on in a new facility in conjunction with the National Park Service. The collections of the park and the society, as well as private collections, will join together to tell the story of the Revolutionary War. This is the world's only museum dedicated to the subject.

THE MARQUEE AT THE PARK. After the bicentennial in 1976, the Valley Forge Historical Society entered into an agreement with the National Park Service to restore and display the Marquee in a special structure inside the visitors center of the Valley Forge National Historical Park. Today, the National Center for the American Revolution, the park, and the historical society are working together to continue to properly care and exhibit the tent.

A BUST OF GEORGE WASHINGTON. Part of the wonderful decorative arts in the collection at Valley Forge is this terra-cotta bust of George Washington by William Rush. It was conserved in the 1980s by the Pennsylvania Academy of Fine Arts for an exhibition featuring a variety of works by Rush.

COMPASS AND SUNDIAL. Acquired from the Washington family, the compass and sundial here once belonged (purportedly) to George Washington. In the collection of the since the 1920s, the artifact is representative of many of the artifacts in the collection in need of conservation. Many objects have been on display for 50 years or more and age.

A MEDICINE CHEST. George Washington's medicine chest traveled with him throughout the campaign of the Revolutionary War. Included in the kit are salve jars, a mortarboard, and variety of bottles and measuring cups. It will be featured along with other Washington-related artifacts in the museum of the National Center for the American Revolution.

A REPRODUCTION HUT. This reproduction hut was the first hut to be constructed Forge in the 20th century. Located to the west of the Washington Memorial Cha constructed in 1905 with funds from the Daughters of the American Revolu it represents a multileveled history of Valley Forge: the actual events of 177 commemorative history, research of the 19th and 20th centuries, and the mo the park in the 21st century.

SELECTED BIBLIOGRAPHY

Burk, Eleanor H.S. *In the Beginning at Valley Forge and the Washington Memorial Cathedral*. North Wales, Pennsylvania: Norman B. Nuss, 1938.

Burk, W. Herbert. "The American Westminster." *DAR Magazine* 42 (1923): 784–787.

———. *Historical and Topographical Guide to Valley Forge*. Norristown, Pennsylvania, 1906. Also published in 1920 and 1928 by Norman B. Nuss, North Wales, Pennsylvania.

———. "Making a Museum: The Confessions of a Curator," 1926.

———. "Valley Forge: Its Past, Present, and Future." *Historical Sketches: A Collection of Papers Prepared for the Historical Society of Montgomery County*, vol. 4 (1910): 235–247.

Powell, Barbara McDonald. "The Most Celebrated Encampment: Valley Forge in American Culture, 1777–1983" (Ph.D. diss., Cornell University, 1983).

Swigart, Stacey A. "The Hanging Rock: Gulph Mills, Pennsylvania." 1997.

———. "The Valley Forge Historical Society," 1998.

———. "Washington Memorial Chapel: Visitors Guide," 1998.

Treese, Lorett. *Valley Forge: Making and Remaking a National Symbol*. Pennsylvania State University Press: University Park, Pennsylvania, 1995.

Valley Forge Historical Society. *The Valley Forge Journal*, 1982–1995.

———. *The Picket Post*, 1943–1981.

"Volunteer Guide." Washington Memorial Chapel. *c.* 1960.

"Washington Memorial Chapel, Guide Book." *c.* 1971.

INDEX